HAL•LEONARD®
VOL. 18

VIOLIN PLAY-ALONG

AUDIO ACCESS INCLUDED

FIDDLE Hymns

T0085330

To access audio visit:
www.halleonard.com/mylibrary

7250-2578-4479-8612

Recorded and Produced by Larry Moore
Violin by Michael Giacobassi

ISBN 978-1-4234-9840-7

In Australia Contact:
Hal Leonard Australia Pty. Ltd.
4 Lentara Court
Cheltenham, Victoria, 3192 Australia
Email: ausadmin@halleonard.com.au

HAL•LEONARD®
CORPORATION
7777 W. BLUEMOUND RD. P.O. BOX 13819 MILWAUKEE, WI 53213

Visit Hal Leonard Online at
www.halleonard.com

HAL•LEONARD®

VIOLIN PLAY-ALONG

AUDIO ACCESS INCLUDED

FIDDLE *Hymns*

VOL. 18

Page	Title
4	Blessed Assurance
6	Down at the Cross (Glory to His Name)
8	He Keeps Me Singing
10	His Eye Is on the Sparrow
22	In the Garden
12	The Old Rugged Cross
14	Since Jesus Came into My Heart
16	Turn Your Eyes upon Jesus
18	Wayfaring Stranger
20	Wonderful Grace of Jesus

Blessed Assurance

Lyrics by Fanny J. Crosby
Music by Phoebe Palmer Knapp

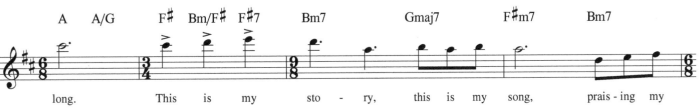

Down at the Cross
(Glory to His Name)

Words by Elisha A. Hoffman
Music by John H. Stockton

Down at the cross where my
I am so won - drous - ly

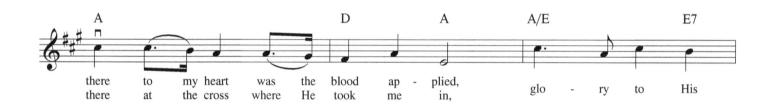

Sav - ior died, down where for cleans - ing from sin I cried;
saved from sin, Je - sus so sweet - ly a - bides with - in;

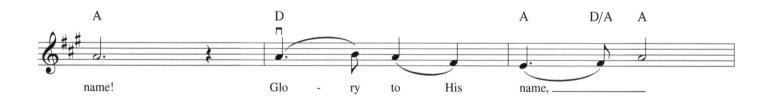

there to my heart was the blood ap - plied, glo - ry to His
there at the cross where He took me in, glo - ry to His

name! Glo - ry to His name, _____

glo - ry to His name! _____ There to my heart was the

blood ap - plied; glo - ry to His name!

name!   *mf*   Come to this foun - tain so rich and sweet,

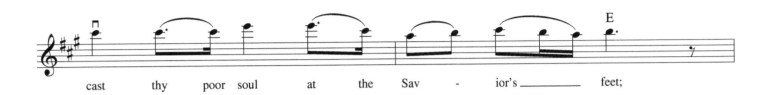

cast thy poor soul at the Sav - ior's _____ feet;

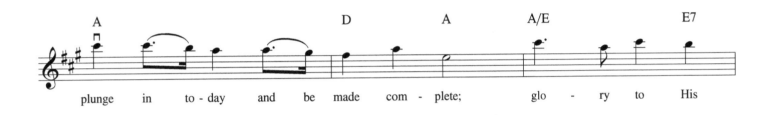

plunge in to - day and be made com - plete; glo - ry to His

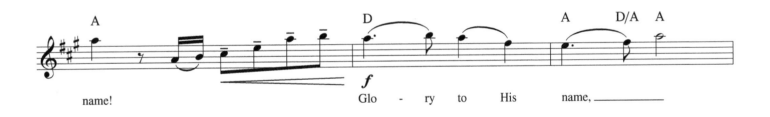

name!   Glo - ry to His name, _____

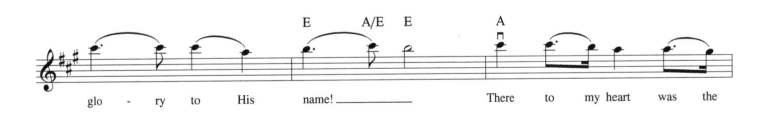

glo - ry to His name! _____ There to my heart was the

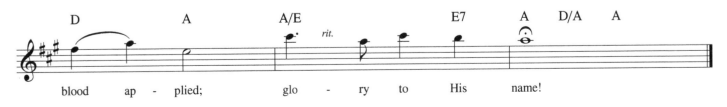

blood ap - plied; glo - ry to His name!

He Keeps Me Singing

Words and Music by Luther B. Bridgers

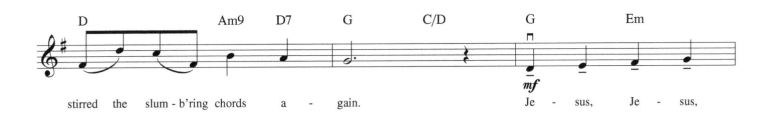

stirred the slum - b'ring chords a - gain. Je - sus, Je - sus,

Je - sus, sweet - est name I know, fills my ev - 'ry

long - ing, keeps me sing - ing as I go.

Soon He's com - ing back to wel - come me far be - yond the star - ry

sky; I shall wing my flight to worlds un - known,

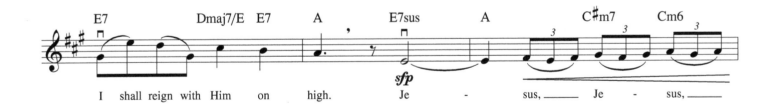

I shall reign with Him on high. Je - sus, Je - sus,

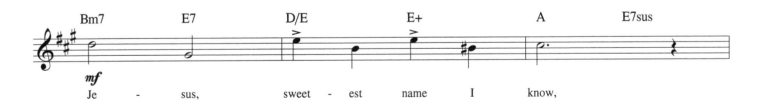

Je - sus, sweet - est name I know,

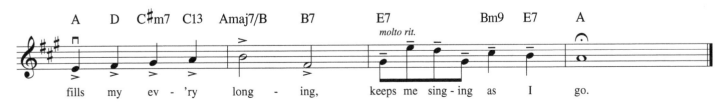

fills my ev - 'ry long - ing, keeps me sing - ing as I go.

9

His Eye Is on the Sparrow

Words by Civilla D. Martin
Music by Charles H. Gabriel

The Old Rugged Cross

Words and Music by Rev. George Bennard

Since Jesus Came into My Heart

Words by Rufus H. McDaniel
Music by Charles H. Gabriel

Moderately (♩ = 92)

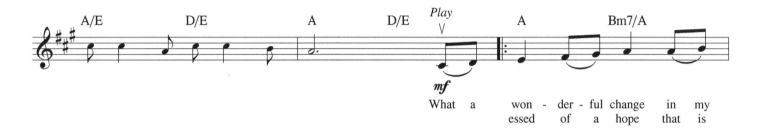

life has been wrought since Je - sus came in - to my heart! I have
stead - fast and sure, since Je - sus came in - to my heart! And no

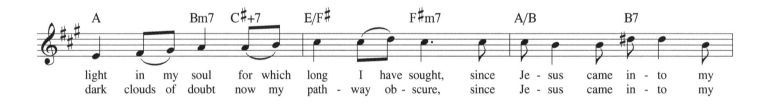

light in my soul for which long I have sought, since Je - sus came in - to my
dark clouds of doubt now my path - way ob - scure, since Je - sus came in - to my

heart! }
heart! } Since Je - sus came in - to my heart, since

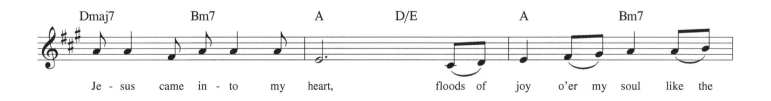

Je - sus came in - to my heart, floods of joy o'er my soul like the

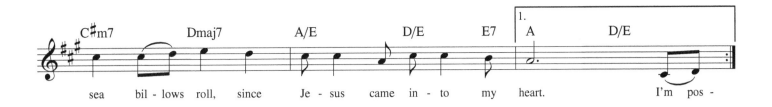

sea bil-lows roll, since Je-sus came in-to my heart. I'm pos-

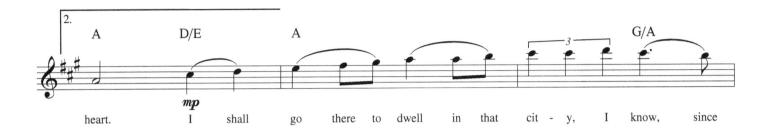

heart. I shall go there to dwell in that cit-y, I know, since

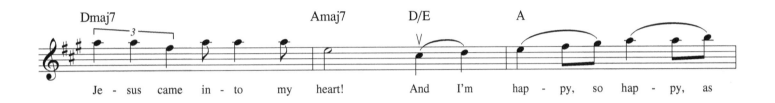

Je-sus came in-to my heart! And I'm hap-py, so hap-py, as

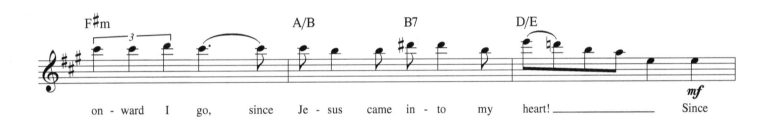

on-ward I go, since Je-sus came in-to my heart! _____ Since

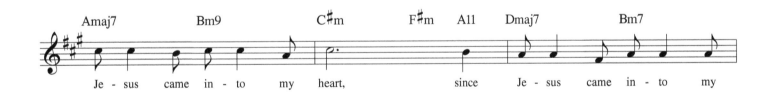

Je-sus came in-to my heart, since Je-sus came in-to my

heart. Floods of joy o'er my soul like the sea bil-lows

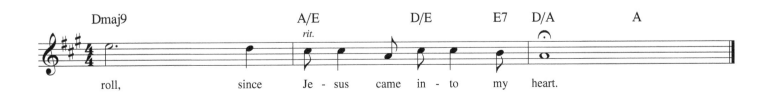

roll, since Je-sus came in-to my heart.

Turn Your Eyes upon Jesus

Words and Music by Helen H. Lemmel

Wayfaring Stranger

Southern American Folk Hymn

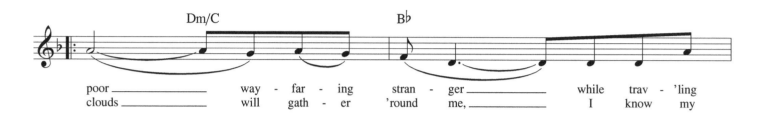

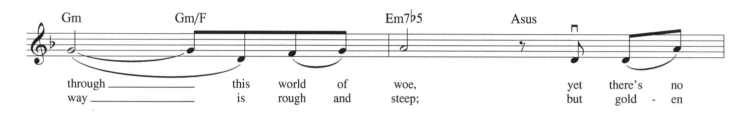

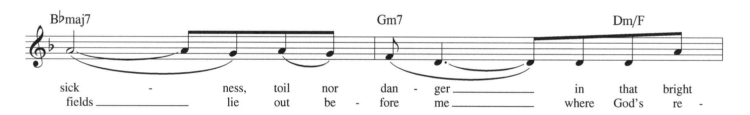

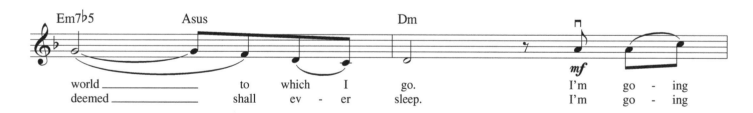

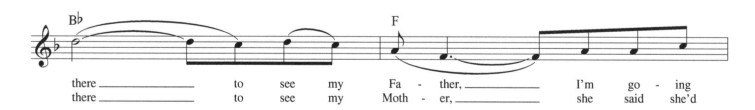

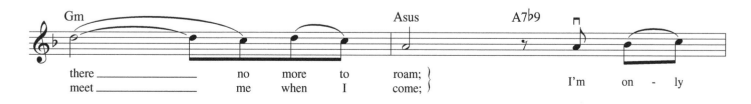

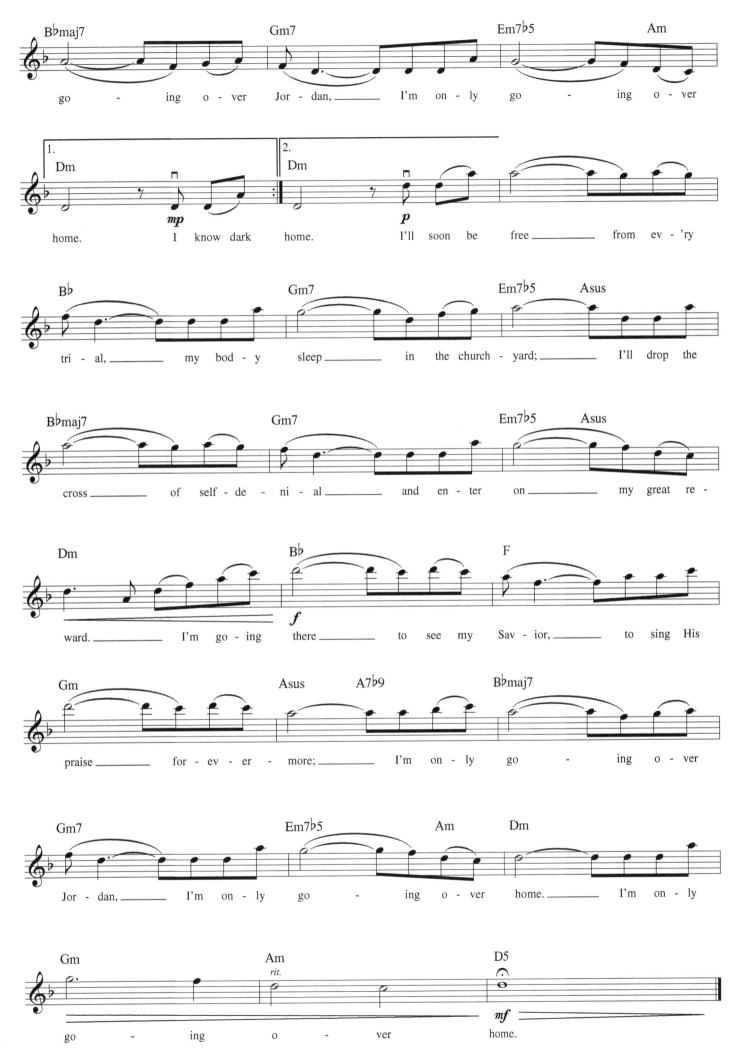

Wonderful Grace of Jesus

Words and Music by Haldor Lillenas

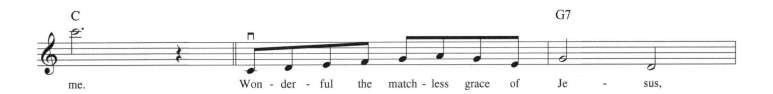

C   G7

me.   Won - der - ful the match - less grace of Je - sus,

C   G7

deep - er than the might - y roll - ing sea.

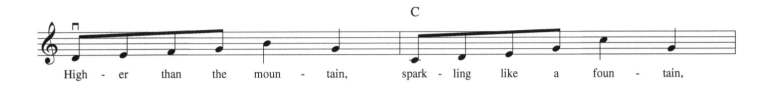

C

High - er than the moun - tain, spark - ling like a foun - tain,

D7   G

all suf - fi - cient grace for e - ven me.

C   G

f

Broad - er than the scope of my trans - gres - sions;

C   C7   F

great - er far than all my sin and shame.   O

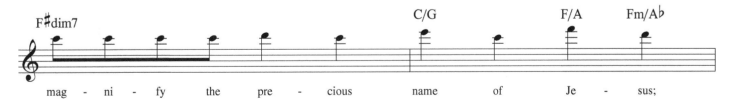

F#dim7   C/G   F/A   Fm/A♭

mag - ni - fy the pre - cious name of Je - sus;

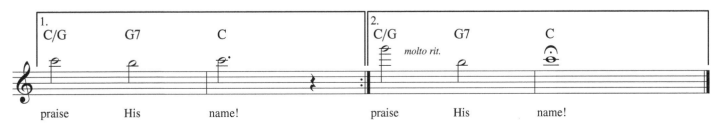

1.   C/G   G7   C   2.   C/G   G7   C

                                                      molto rit.

praise His name!   praise His name!

In the Garden

Words and Music by C. Austin Miles

HAL•LEONARD® VIOLIN PLAY-ALONG

AUDIO ACCESS INCLUDED

The Violin Play-Along Series

Play your favorite songs quickly and easily!

Just follow the music, listen to the CD or online audio to hear how the violin should sound, and then play along using the separate backing tracks. The audio files are enhanced so you can adjust the recordings to any tempo without changing pitch!

1. Bluegrass
00842152 ....$14.99

2. Popular Songs
00842153 ....$16.99

3. Classical
00842154 ....$16.99

4. Celtic
00842155 ....$14.99

5. Christmas Carols
00842156 ....$14.99

6. Classic Christmas Songs
00348311 ....$14.99

7. Jazz
00842196 ....$16.99

8. Country Classics
00842230 ....$14.99

9. Country Hits
00842231 ....$14.99

10. Bluegrass Favorites
00842232 ....$14.99

11. Bluegrass Classics
00842233 ....$16.99

12. Wedding Classics
00842324 ....$14.99

13. Wedding Favorites
00842325 ....$16.99

14. Blues Classics
00842427 ....$14.99

15. Stephane Grappelli
00842428 ....$16.99

16. Folk Songs
00842429 ....$14.99

17. Christmas Favorites
00842478 ....$14.99

18. Fiddle Hymns
00842499 ....$16.99

19. Lennon & McCartney
00842564 ....$14.99

20. Irish Tunes
00842565 ....$16.99

21. Andrew Lloyd Webber
00842566 ....$16.99

22. Broadway Hits
00842567 ....$14.99

23. Pirates of the Caribbean
00842625 ....$16.99

24. Rock Classics
00842640 ....$14.99

25. Classical Masterpieces
00842642 ....$14.99

26. Elementary Classics
00842643 ....$14.99

27. Classical Favorites
00842646 ....$14.99

28. Classical Treasures
00842647 ....$14.99

29. Disney Favorites
00842648 ....$16.99

30. Disney Hits
00842649 ....$14.99

31. Movie Themes
00842706 ....$14.99

32. Favorite Christmas Songs
00102110 ....$14.99

33. Hoedown
00102161 ....$14.99

34. Barn Dance
00102568 ....$14.99

35. Lindsey Stirling
00109715 ....$19.99

36. Hot Jazz
00110373 ....$14.99

37. Taylor Swift
00116361 ....$14.99

38. John Williams
00116367 ....$16.99

39. Italian Songs
00116368 ....$14.99

40. Trans-Siberian Orchestra
00119909 ....$19.99

41. Johann Strauss
00121041 ....$14.99

42. Light Classics
00121935 ....$14.99

43. Light Orchestra Pop
00122126 ....$14.99

44. French Songs
00122123 ....$14.99

45. Lindsey Stirling Hits
00123128 ....$19.99

46. Piazzolla Tangos
48022997 ....$16.99

47. Light Masterworks
00124149 ....$14.99

48. Frozen
00126478 ....$14.99

49. Pop/Rock
00130216 ....$14.99

50. Songs for Beginners
00131417 ....$14.99

51. Chart Hits for Beginners – 2nd Ed.
00293887 ....$14.99

52. Celtic Rock
00148756 ....$16.99

53. Rockin' Classics
00148768 ....$14.99

54. Scottish Folksongs
00148779 ....$14.99

55. Wicked
00148780 ....$14.99

56. The Sound of Music
00148782 ....$14.99

57. Movie Music
00150962 ....$14.99

58. The Piano Guys – Wonders
00151837 ....$19.99

59. Worship Favorites
00152534 ....$16.99

60. The Beatles
00155293 ....$16.99

61. Star Wars: The Force Awakens
00157648 ....$14.99

62. Star Wars
00157650 ....$16.99

63. George Gershwin
00159612 ....$14.99

64. Lindsey Stirling Favorites
00159634 ....$19.99

65. Taylor Davis
00190208 ....$19.99

66. Pop Covers
00194642 ....$14.99

67. Love Songs
00211896 ....$14.99

68. Queen
00221964 ....$14.99

69. La La Land
00232247 ....$17.99

70. Metallica
00242929 ....$14.99

71. Andrew Lloyd Webber Hits
00244688 ....$14.99

72. Lindsey Stirling – Selections from Warmer in the Winter
00254923 ....$19.99

73. Taylor Davis Favorites
00256297 ....$19.99

74. The Piano Guys – Christmas Together
00262873 ....$19.99

75. Ed Sheeran
00274194 ....$16.99

76. Cajun & Zydeco Songs
00338131 ....$14.99

77. Favorite Christmas Hymns
00278017 ....$14.99

78. Hillsong Worship Hits
00279512 ....$14.99

79. Lindsey Stirling – Top Songs
00284305 ....$19.99

80. Gypsy Jazz
00293922 ....$14.99

81. Lindsey Stirling – Christmas Collection
00298588 ....$19.99

HAL•LEONARD®

www.halleonard.com